WITCHCRAFT

AND

DEVIL LORE

IN THE

CHANNEL ISLANDS

TRANSCRIPTS FROM THE OFFICIAL RECORDS OF
THE GUERNSEY ROYAL COURT, WITH AN
ENGLISH TRANSLATION AND HISTORICAL
INTRODUCTION.

BY

JOHN LINWOOD PITTS,

Membre de la Société des Antiquaires de Normandie.

*Editor of "The Patois Poems of the Channel Islands;" "The
Sermon on the Mount and the Parable of the Sower, in the
Franco-Norman Dialects of Guernsey and Sark," &c., &c.*

1

Thou shalt not suffer a witch to live.

—EXODUS xxii, 18.

1886.

TO

EDGAR MacCULLOCH, Esquire,

F.S.A., LONDON AND NORMANDY, AND MEMBER
OF THE FOLKLORE SOCIETY,

BAILIFF OF GUERNSEY,

WHOSE HISTORICAL RESEARCHES HAVE
TENDED SO MUCH TO ELUCIDATE THE TIME-
HONOURED CONSTITUTION

AND

ANCIENT CUSTOMS OF HIS NATIVE ISLAND,

THIS

BRIEF RECORD OF ONE OF THE DARKEST
CHAPTERS IN ITS CHEQUERED ANNALS

IS DEDICATED

WITH SENTIMENTS OF THE HIGHEST RESPECT
AND ESTEEM.

Venena magnum fas nefasque non valent Convertere humanam vicem.

HORACE, Epod. V. 87-8.

FOREWORD.

In presenting to the public another little volume of the "Guille-Allès Library Series," it affords me much pleasure to acknowledge various kindnesses experienced during its preparation. From Edgar MacCulloch, Esq., F.S.A., Bailiff of Guernsey, I have received several valuable hints and suggestions bearing upon the subject; and also from F.J. Jérémie, Esq., M.A., Jurat of the Royal Court. I am also particularly indebted to James Gallienne, Esq., Her Majesty's Greffier, for his uniform kindness and courtesy in allowing the fullest access at all times to the Archives under his care, not only in respect to the subject-matter of the present publication, but also in other historical researches which I have wished to make. I am equally obliged to Mr. E.M. Cohu and Mr. H.J.V. Torode, Deputy-Greffiers, and to Mr. A. Isemonger, Bailiff's Clerk, for various information and much ready help, which materially facilitated my investigations. All these gentlemen have my cordial acknowledgments and best thanks.

J.L.P.

Guernsey, December, 1885.

NOTE.—The Seal represented on the title page is that of the Guernsey Bailiwick. It was first granted by Edward I. in the seventh year of his reign (1279), and bears the inscription: S. BALLIVIE INSULE DE GERNEREYE.

INTRODUCTION.

The Witchcraft superstitions of the Channel Islands, sad as they were in their characteristics and results—as is abundantly evidenced by our judicial records—were but a part and parcel of that vast wave of unreasoning credulity which swept across the civilised world during the Middle Ages, and more or less affected every class of society, and all sorts and conditions of men. From the lists given in the following pages, it will be seen that in about seventy-one years, during the reigns of Elizabeth, James I. and Charles I., no fewer than seventy-eight persons—fifty-eight of them being women, and twenty of them men—were brought to trial for Sorcery in Guernsey alone. Out of these unfortunate victims, three women and one man appear to have been burnt alive; twenty-four women and four men were hanged first and burnt afterwards; one woman was hanged for returning to the island after being banished; three women and one man were whipped and had each an ear cut off; twenty-two women and five men were banished from the island; while five women and three men had the good fortune to be acquitted. Most of these accused persons were natives of Guernsey, but mention is made of one woman from Jersey, of three men and a woman from Sark, and of a man from Alderney.

With regard to the gatherings at the so-called Witches' Sabbaths, there can be no doubt that—quite apart from the question of any diabolic presence at such meetings—very questionable assemblies of people did take place at intervals among the inhabitants of many countries. Probably these gatherings first had their rise in the old pagan times, and were subsequently continued from force of habit, long after their real origin and significance had been forgotten.[Pg 2] Now, it would be very easy for these orgies to become

11

associated—particularly in the then superstitious condition of the popular mind—with the actual bodily presence of the Devil as one of the participants; while it is also not improbable that, in some cases at least, heartless and evil-minded persons worked upon the prevailing credulity to further their own nefarious purposes. Our esteemed Bailiff has offered a suggestion or two of considerable value on this point with regard to certain Guernsey phases of the superstition. He thinks it highly probable that some of these deluded women were actually the dupes of unprincipled and designing men, who arrayed themselves in various disguises and then met their unfortunate victims by appointment. This idea is, indeed, borne out to a great extent by some of the particulars stated in the following confessions. For instance, some of the women assert that when they met the Devil he was in the form of a dog, *but rather larger*, he always stood upon his hind legs—probably the man's feet; and, when he shook hands with them, his paw *felt like a hand*—doubtless it *was* a hand. Another suggestion of the Bailiff's is also worth notice. It is that the black ointment so often mentioned as being rubbed on the bodies of the so-called witches, had a real existence, and may have been so compounded as to act as a narcotic or intoxicant, and produce a kind of extatic condition, just as the injection of certain drugs beneath the skin is known to do now. These suggestions are certainly worth consideration as offering reasonable solutions of at least two difficulties connected with those strange and lamentable superstitions. In one way or other there must have been some physical basis for beliefs so widely extended and so terribly real. Imagination, of course, possesses a marvellous power of modification and exaggeration, but still it requires some germs of fact around which to crystallise. And it is to the discovery of the nature of such germs that a careful and conscientious observer will naturally turn his attention.

While speaking of the burning of Witches in Guernsey,[Pg 3] I may also refer for a moment to the three women who, in Queen Mary's reign suffered death by fire, for heresy, because the reason of their condemnation and punishment has caused some controversy, and is often associated in the popular mind with a charge of sorcery. Dr. Heylin in his *Survey* (page 323), says:—

Katherine Gowches, a poor woman of St. Peter-Port, in Guernsey, was noted to be much absent from church, and her two daughters guilty of the same neglect. Upon this they were presented before James Amy, then dean of the island, who, finding in them that they held opinions contrary to those then allowed about the sacrament of the altar, pronounced them heretics, and condemned them to the fire. The poor women, on the other side, pleaded for themselves, that that doctrine had been taught them in the time of King Edward; but if the queen was otherwise disposed, they were content to be of her religion. This was fair but it would not serve; for by the dean they were delivered unto Helier Gosselin, then bailiff, and by him unto the fire, July 18, 1556. One of these daughters, Perotine Massey, she was called, was at that time great with child; her husband, who was a minister, having in those dangerous times fled the island; in the middle of the flames and anguish of her torments, her belly broke in sunder, and her child, a goodly boy, fell down into the fire, but was presently snatched up by one W. House, one of the by-standers. Upon the noise of this strange incident, the cruel bailiff returned command that the poor infant must be cast again into the flames, which was accordingly performed; and so that pretty babe was born a martyr, and added to the number of the holy innocents.

Parsons, the English Jesuit, has asserted that the women were felons and were executed for theft, while other apologists have described them as prostitutes and generally infamous in character. The original sentences, however, which still exist at the Guernsey *Greffe*, and which I have examined, conclusively settle the question. Both the ecclesiastical sentence, which is in Latin, and the civil sentence, which is in French, distinctly describe the charge as one of *heresy*, and make no mention whatever of any other crime as having aught to do with the condemnation.

It has been questioned too whether a child could be born alive under such circumstances. Mr. F.B. Tupper, in his *History of Guernsey* (page 151), says: "We are assured by competent surgical authority that the case is very possible"; and he further mentions that in a volume entitled *Three Visits to Madagascar*, by the Rev. Wm. Ellis, published in London, in 1858, a precisely similar[Pg 4] case is stated to have occurred in that island. A native woman was burnt for becoming a convert to Christianity, and her infant, born in the flames, was thrust into them again, and burnt also.

Lord Tennyson refers to this Guernsey martyrdom in his historical drama of *Queen Mary* (Act v. Scene iv.). It is night-time in London; a light is burning in the Royal Palace; and he makes two "Voices of the Night" say:—

First:—There's the Queen's light. I hear she cannot live.

Second:—God curse her and her Legate! Gardiner burns

Already; but to pay them full in kind,
The hottest hold in all the devil's den
Were but a sort of winter; Sir, in Guernsey,
I watch'd a woman burn; and in her agony
The mother came upon her—a child was born—
And, Sir, they hurl'd it back into the fire,

That, being thus baptised in fire, the babe
Might be in fire for ever. Ah, good neighbour,
There should be something fierier than fire
To yield them their deserts.

With regard to Witchcraft in Jersey, I have not had an
opportunity of personally examining the official records
there. I find, however, some information on the subject,
given by M. De La Croix, in his *Ville de St. Hélier*, and *Les
Etats de Jersey*, upon which I have drawn. In the way of
legislation, the Guernsey Court does not appear to have
promulgated any penal statutes on the subject, being content
to treat the crime as one against the common law of the
Island. In Jersey on the contrary, Witchcraft was specially
legislated against at least on one occasion, for we find that on
December 23rd, 1591, the Royal Court of that island passed
an Ordinance, of which the following is the purport:—

Forasmuch as many persons have hitherto committed and
perpetrated great and grievous faults, as well against the
honour and express commandment of God as to the great
scandal of the Christian faith, and of those who are charged
with the administration of justice, by seeking assistance from
Witches and Diviners in their ills and afflictions; and seeing
that ignorance is no excuse for sin, and that no one can tell
what vice and danger may ensue from such practices: This
Act declares that for the time to come everyone shall turn
away from such iniquitous and diabolical practices, against
which the law of God decrees the same punishments as
against Witches and Enchanters themselves; and also in[Pg
*4] order that the Divine Vengeance may be averted, which
on account of the impunity with which these crimes have
been committed, now threatens those who have the
repression of them in their hands. It is, therefore, strictly
forbidden to all the inhabitants of this island to receive any
counsel or assistance in their adversities from any Witches
or Diviners, or anyone suspected of practicing Sorcery,

under pain of one month's imprisonment in the Castle, on bread and water; and on their liberation they shall declare to the Court the cause of such presumption, and according as this shall appear reasonable, shall be dealt with as the law of God directs.

In 1562 two women were executed in Jersey for witchcraft. One of them named *Anne*, a native of St. Brelade's, was burnt at St. Helier's; and the other, *Michelle La Blanche*, expiated her crime at the gibbet of the Hurets, in the parish of St. Ouen, because criminals dwelling on the Fief Haubert de St. Ouen, were, in accordance with custom, required to be executed within the boundaries of the said Fief—seeing that it possessed a gallows-right—and their goods and lands became forfeited to the Seigneur.

In 1583 a rather curious point of law was raised in connection with a pending witch-trial at St. Helier's. On the 15th of February in that year, a suspected witch named *Marion Corbel*, who had been imprisoned in the Castle awaiting her trial, suddenly died. Whereupon her relatives came forward and claimed to be heirs to her goods and chattels, seeing that she had not been convicted of the imputed crime, and urging that her death put an end to further criminal proceedings. The Queen's Procureur, however—it was in the reign of Elizabeth—contended that death was no bar to the completion of the indictment, although it had effectually removed the criminal from the jurisdiction of the Court, as far as punishment was concerned. The very reasonable claim of the deceased woman's relatives was therefore set aside, and the defunct of course being found guilty, her possessions reverted to the crown.

Again, forty years later, in 1623, an old woman of sixty, named *Marie Filleul,* daughter of *Thomas Filleul,* of the parish of St. Clement's, was tried before a jury of twenty-four of her countrymen, and found guilty of the diabolical crime of Sorcery. She was therefore hanged and burnt as a witch, and her goods were confiscated to the King [James I.], and to the Seigneurs to whom they belonged.

It may be interesting to note here the opinion of Mr. Philippe Le Geyt, the famous commentator on the constitution and laws of Jersey, and one of the most enlightened men of his time, who for many years was Lieutenant-Bailiff of that island. He was born in 1635 and died in 1715, in his eighty-first year. In Vol. I., page 42, of his works, there occurs a passage of which the following is a translation:—

As Holy Scripture forbids us to allow witches to live, many persons have made it a matter of conscience and of religion to be severe in respect to such a crime. This principle has without doubt made many persons credulous. How often have purely accidental associations been taken as convincing proofs? How many innocent people have perished in the flames on the asserted testimony of supernatural circumstances? I will not say that there are no witches; but ever since the difficulty of convicting them has been recognized in the island, they all seem to have disappeared, as though the evidence of the times gone by had been but an illusion. This shows the instability of all things here below.

Coming down now to within a century ago, we find an article in the *Gazette de Jersey*, of Saturday, March 10th, 1787, complaining of the great increase of wizards and witches in the island, as well as of their supposed victims. The writer says that the scenes then taking place were truly ridiculous, and he details a case that had just occurred at St. Brelade's as corroborative of his assertion. It appears that a worthy householder there, had dreamed that a certain wizard appeared to him and ordered him to poison himself at a date which was specified, enjoining him above all things not to mention the incident to anyone. The poor silly fellow was dreadfully distressed, for he felt convinced that he would have to carry out the disagreeable command. At the same time he was quite unable to keep so momentous a secret to himself, and so he divulged the approaching tragedy to his wife. The good woman's despair was fully equal to his own, and after much anxious domestic counsel they determined to seek the good offices of a White Witch (*une Quéraude*), with the hope that her incantations might overcome the evil spells of the Black Witch who was causing all the mischief. This White Witch prescribed lengthened fasting and other preparations for the great ordeal, and on a given night she and the bewitched householder, together with his wife and four or five trusty friends with drawn swords, shut themselves up in a room, and commenced their mysterious ceremonial. There was the boiling of occult herbs; the roasting of a beeve's heart stuck full of nails and pins; the reading of certain passages from the family Bible; a mighty gesticulating with the swords, which were first thrust up the chimney to prevent the Black Witch from coming down, and anon were pointed earthward to hinder him from rising up; and so the ridiculous game went on. The only person who benefited was of course the imposter, who was paid for her services; while we may perhaps charitably hope that her dupes also were afterwards easier in their minds. The writer adds that many other persons besides this man at St. Brelade's, had latterly believed themselves bewitched, and had consulted wizards, who were thus driving a profitable trade.

Among the indications and symptoms of a witch, are reckoned various bodily marks and spots, said to be insensible to pain, inability to shed tears, &c. The pricking of witches was at one time a lucrative profession both in

England and Scotland, one of the most noted prickers being a wretched imposter named Matthew Hopkins who was sent for to all parts of the country to exercise his vile art. Ralph Gardner, in his *England's Grievance Discovered* (1655), speaks also of two prickers, Thomas Shovel and Cuthbert Nicholson, who, in 1649 and 1650, were sent by the magistrates of Newcastle-on-Tyne, into Scotland, there to confer with another very able man in that line and bring him back to Newcastle. They were to have twenty shillings, but the Scotchman three pounds, per head *of all they could convict,* and a free passage there and back. When these wretches got to any town—for they tried all the chief market-towns in the district—the crier used to go round with his bell, desiring "all people that would bring in any complaint against any woman for a witch, they should be sent for and tried by the person appointed." As many as thirty women were brought at[Pg 6] once into the Newcastle town-hall, stripped and pricked, and twenty-seven set aside as guilty. Gardner continues:—

The said witch-finder acquainted Lieutenant-Colonel Hobson that he knew women whether they were witches or no by their looks; and when the said person was searching of a personable and good-like woman, the said colonel replied and said, 'Surely this woman is none, and need not be tried;' but the Scotchman said she was, for the town said she was, and therefore he would try her; and presently, in sight of all the people, laid her body naked to the waist, with her clothes over her head, by which fright and shame all her blood contracted into one part of her body, and then he ran a pin into her thigh, and then suddenly let her coats fall, and then demanded whether she had nothing of his in her body, but did not bleed? But she, being amazed, replied little. Then he put his hands up her coats and pulled out the pin, and set her aside as a guilty person and child of the devil, and fell to try others, whom he made guilty. Lieutenant-Colonel Hobson, perceiving the alteration of the aforesaid woman by her blood settling in her right parts, caused that woman to be brought again, and her clothes pulled up to her thigh, and required the Scot to run the pin into the same place, and then it gushed out of blood, and the said Scot cleared her, and said she was not a child of the devil.

If this precious wretch had not been stopped he would have declared half the women in the north country to be witches. But the magistrates and the people got tired of him at last, and his imposture being discovered, he was hanged in Scotland. At the gallows he confessed that he had been the death of 220 men and women in England and Scotland, simply for the sake of the twenty shillings which he generally received as blood-money.

The belief in *Sorcerots*, or witches' spells of a peculiar kind, mentioned in the *Depositions* receives curious modern confirmation by a kindred superstition still current among the emancipated negroes of the United States. It was described in a letter on "Voudouism in Virginia" which appeared in the *New York Tribune*, dated Richmond, September 17, 1875. Mr. Moncure D. Conway, in quoting this and commenting on it in his *Demonology and Devil-Lore*, says that it belongs to a class of superstitions generally kept close from the whites, as he believes, because of their purely African origin. Mr. Conway is, however, probably mistaken about the origin, seeing that the same belief prevailed in Guernsey three centuries ago. The extract from the letter is as follows:—

If an ignorant negro is smitten with a disease which he cannot comprehend, he often imagines himself the victim of witchcraft, and having no faith in "white folks' physic" for such ailments, must apply to one of these quacks. A physician residing near the city [Richmond] was invited by such a one to witness his mode of procedure with a dropsical patient for whom the physician in question had occasionally charitably prescribed. Curiosity led him to attend the seance, having previously informed the quack that since the case was in such hands he relinquished all connection with it. On the coverlet of the bed on which the sick man lay, was spread a quantity of bones, feathers, and other trash. The charlatan went through with a series of so-called conjurations, burned feathers, hair, and tiny fragments of wood in a charcoal furnace, and mumbled gibberish past the physician's comprehension. He then proceeded to rip open the pillows and bolsters, and took from them some queer conglomerations of feathers. These he said had caused all the trouble. Sprinkling a whitish powder over them, he burnt them in his furnace. A black offensive smoke was produced, and he announced triumphantly that the evil influence was destroyed, and that the patient would surely get well. He died not many days later, believing, in common with his friends and relatives, that the conjurations of the "trick doctor" had failed to save him only because resorted to too late.

From the above it is evident that the natural tendency of wool and feathers to felt and clog together, has been distorted, by widely different peoples, into an outward and visible sign that occult and malignant influences were at work.

As to the manner in which wizards and witches were put to the question in Guernsey—that is tortured until they confessed whatever was required of them—Mr. Warburton, a herald and celebrated antiquary who wrote in the reign of Charles II., has given a circumstancial account, the correctness of which may be relied on. His *Treatise on the History, Laws and Customs of the Island of Guernsey*, bears the date of 1682, and at page 126 he says:—

By the law approved (*Terrien*, Lib. xii. cap. 37), torture is to be used, though not upon slight presumption, yet where the presumptive proof is strong, and much more when the proof is positive, and there wants only the confession of the party accused. Yet this practice of torturing does not appear to have been used in the island for some ages, except in the case of witches, when it was too frequently applied, near a century since. The custom then was, when any person was supposed guilty of sorcery or witchcraft, they carried them to a place in the town called *La Tour Beauregard*, and there, tying their hands behind them by the two thumbs, drew them to a certain height with an engine made for that purpose, by which means sometimes their shoulders were turned round; and sometimes their thumbs torn off; but this fancy of witches has for some years been laid aside.

It will be noticed in the subsequent *Confessions* of witches (page 11, &c.), that a number of colons (:) are[Pg 7] inserted in the text where they would not be required as ordinary marks of punctuation. These correspond, however, to similar pauses in the original records, and evidently indicate the successive stages by which the story was wrung from the wretched victims. They are thus endowed with a sad and ghastly significance, which must be borne in mind when the confessions are read. It must also be remembered that these confessions were not usually made in the connected form in which they stand recorded, but were rather the result of leading questions put by the inquisitors, such as: How old were you when the Devil first appeared to you? What form did he assume? What parish were you in? What were you doing? &c., &c.

Melancholy and revolting as all this is, yet the tortures made use of in Guernsey were far from possessing those refinements of cruelty and that intensity of brutality which characterised the methods practiced in some other countries. Let us take as a proof of this, the notable case of Dr. Fian and his associates, who were tried at Edinburgh, in the year 1591. The evidence was of the usual ridiculous kind, and a confession—afterwards withdrawn—was extorted by the following blood-curdling barbarities, as is quoted by Mr. C.K. Sharpe, in his *Historical Account of the Belief in Witchcraft in Scotland*:—

The said Doctor was taken and imprisoned, and used with the accustomed paine provided for those offences inflicted upon the rest, as is aforesaid. First, by thrawing of his head with a rope, whereat he would confesse nothing. Secondly, he was perswaded by faire meanes to confesse his follies; but that would prevaile as little. Lastly, hee was put to the most severe and cruell paine in the world, called the bootes, who, after he had received three strokes, being inquired if he would confesse his damnable actes and wicked life, his toong would not serve him to speak; in respect whereof, the rest of the witches willed to search his toong, under which was founde two pinnes thrust up into the heade, whereupon the witches did say, now is the charme stinted, and shewed that these charmed pins were the cause he could not confesse any thing; then was he immediately released of the bootes, brought before the King, his confession was taken, and his own hand willingly set thereunto.... But this Doctor, notwithstanding that his owne confession appeareth remaining in recorde under his owne hande-writing, and the same thereunto fixed in the presence of the King's majestie, and sundrie of his councell, yet did he utterly denie the same. Whereupon the Kinges majestie, perceiving his stubbourne wilfulnesse, conceived and imagined that in the time of his absence hee had entered into newe conference and league with the devill, his master, and that hee had[Pg *7] beene

23

agayne newly marked, for the which he was narrowly searched; but it coulde not in anie wice be founde; yet, for more tryall of him to make him confesse, hee was commaunded to have a most straunge torment, which was done in this manner following: His nailes upon all his fingers were riven and pulled off with an instrument called in Scottish a turkas, which in England wee call a payre of pincers, and under everie nayle there was thrust in two needles over, even up to the heads; at all which tormentes notwithstanding the Doctor never shronke anie whit, neither woulde he then confesse it the sooner for all the tortures inflicted upon him. Then was hee, with all convenient speed, by commandement, convaied againe to the torment of the bootes, wherein he continued a long time, and did abide so many blowes in them, that the legges were crusht and beaten together as small as might bee, and the bones and flesh so bruised that the blood and marrow spouted forth in great abundance, whereby they were made unserviceable for ever; and notwithstanding all those grievous paines and cruell torments, hee would not confess anie thing; so deeply had the devill entered into his heart, that hee utterly denied all that which he had before avouched, and would saie nothing thereunto but this, that what he had done and sayde before, was onely done and sayde for fear of paynes which he had endured. After this horrible treatment the wretched man was strangled and burnt.

The following list gives a few—and only a few—of the direful results to which this widespread superstition led. The instances are chiefly taken from Dr. Réville's *History of the Devil*, and Haydn's well-known *Dictionary of Dates*:—

At Toulouse a noble lady, fifty-six years of age, named Angela de Labarète, was the first who was burnt as a sorceress, in which special quality she formed part of the great *auto-da-fé* which took place in that city in the year 1275; at Carcasonne, from 1320 to 1350, more than four hundred

24

executions for witchcraft are on record; in 1309 many Templars were burnt at Paris for witchcraft; Joan of Arc was burnt as a witch at Rouen, May 30th, 1431; in 1484 Pope Innocent VIII. issued a bull against witchcraft, causing persecutions to break out in all parts of Christendom; during three months of the year 1515, about five hundred witches were burnt at Geneva; in 1524 many persons were burnt for the same crime in the Diocese of Como; about the year 1520 a great number suffered in France, and one sorcerer confessed to having 1,200 associates; from 1580 to 1595—a period of fifteen years—about nine hundred witches were burnt in Lorraine; between 1627 and 1629, no fewer than one hundred and fifty-seven persons, old and young, and of all ranks, were burnt at Wurtzburg, in Bavaria; in 1634 a clerk named Urbain Grandier, who was parish priest at Loudon, was burnt on a charge of having bewitched a whole convent of Ursuline nuns; in 1654 twenty poor women were put to death as witches in Brittany; in 1648-9 serious disturbances on account of witchcraft took place in Massachusetts; and in 1683 dreadful persecutions raged in Pennsylvania from the same cause; in 1692, at Salem, in New England, nineteen persons were hanged by the Puritans for witchcraft, and eight more were condemned, while fifty others confessed themselves to be witches, and were pardoned; in 1657 the witch-judge Nicholas Remy boasted of having burnt nine hundred persons in fifteen years; in one German principality alone, at least two hundred and forty-two persons were burnt between 1646 and 1651, including many children from one to six years of age; in 1749 Maria Renata was burnt at Wurtzburg for witchcraft; on January 17th,[Pg 8] 1775, nine old women were burnt at Kalish, in Poland, on a charge of having bewitched and rendered unfruitful the lands belonging to the palatinate; at Landshut, in Bavaria, in 1756, a young girl of thirteen years was convicted of impure intercourse with the Devil and put to death. There were also executions for sorcery at Seville, in

Spain, in 1781, and at Glarus, in Switzerland, in 1783; while even as late as December 15th, 1802, five women were condemned to death for sorcery at Patna, in the Bengal Presidency, by the Brahmins, and were all executed.

IN ENGLAND the record of Witchcraft is also a melancholy chapter. A statute was enacted declaring all witchcraft and sorcery to be felony without benefit of clergy, 33 Henry VIII. 1541; and again 5 Elizabeth, 1562, and 1 James I. 1603. The 73rd Canon of the Church, 1603, prohibits the Clergy from casting out devils. Barrington estimates the judicial murders for witchcraft in England, during two hundred years, at 30,000; Matthew Hopkins, the "witch-finder," caused the judicial murder of about one hundred persons in Essex, Norfolk, and Suffolk, 1645-7; Sir Matthew Hale burnt two persons for witchcraft in 1664; about 1676 seventeen or eighteen persons were burnt as witches at St. Osyths, in Essex; in 1705 two pretended witches were executed at Northampton, and five others seven years afterwards; in 1716, a Mrs. Hicks, and her daughter, a little girl of nine years old, are said to have been hanged as witches at Huntingdon, but of this there seems to be some doubt. The last really authentic trial in England for witchcraft took place in 1712, when the jury convicted an old woman named Jane Wenham, of Walkerne, a little village in the north of Hertfordshire, and she was sentenced to be hanged. The judge, however, quietly procured a reprieve for her, and a kind-hearted gentleman in the neighbourhood gave her a cottage to live in, where she ended her days in peace. With regard to the mobbing of reputed sorcerers, it is recorded that in the year 1628, Dr. Lamb, a so-called wizard, who had been under the protection of the Duke of Buckingham, was torn to pieces by a London mob. While even as late as April 22nd, 1751, a wild and tossing rabble of about 5,000 persons beset and broke into the work-house at Tring, in Hertfordshire, where seizing Luke Osborne and his wife, two inoffensive old people suspected of witchcraft, they

26

ducked them in a pond till the old woman died. After which, her corpse was put to bed to her husband by the mob, of whom only one person—a chimney-sweeper named Colley, who was the ringleader—was brought to trial and hanged for the detestable outrage.

The laws against witchcraft in England had lain dormant for many years, when an ignorant person attempted to revive them by filing a bill against a poor old woman in Surrey, accused as a witch; this led to the repeal of the laws by the statute 10 George II. 1736. Credulity in witchcraft, however, still lingers in some of the country districts of the United Kingdom. On September 4th, 1863, a poor old paralysed Frenchman died in consequence of having been ducked as a wizard at Castle Hedingham, in Essex, and similar cases have since occurred; while on September 17th, 1875,—only ten years ago—an old woman named Ann Turner, was killed as a witch, by a half-insane man, at Long Compton, Warwickshire.

IN SCOTLAND, thousands of persons were burnt for witchcraft within a period of about a hundred years, in the fifteenth and sixteenth centuries. Among the victims were persons of the highest rank, while all orders of the state concurred. James I. even caused a whole assize to be prosecuted because of an acquittal; the king published his work on *Dæmonologie*, in Edinburgh, in 1597; the last sufferer for witchcraft in Scotland was at Dornoch, in 1722.

CONFESSIONS OF WITCHES UNDER TORTURE.

LE 4 JUILLET 1617.

Devant AMICE DE CARTERET, Ecuyer, Baillif, présents, etc.

SENTENCE DE MORT.

Collette Du Mont, veuve de *Jean Becquet, Marie,* sa fille, femme de *Pierre Massy, Isbel Bequet,* femme de *Jean Le Moygne,* etant par la coutume renommée et bruit des gens de longue main du bruit de damnable art de Sorcellerie, et icelles sur ce saisies et apprehendées par les Officiers de Sa Majesté, apres s'etre volontairement sumis et sur l'enquete generale du pays, et apres avoir été plusieurs fois conduites en Justice, ouïes, examinées et confrontées sur un grand nombre de depositions faites et produites à l'encontre d'elles par les dits Officiers, par lesquels est clair et evident qu'auraient, par longeur d'années, le susdit diabolique art de Sorcellerie, par avoir non seulement jété leur sort sur des choses insensible, mais aussi tenu en langueur par maladies etranges plusieurs personnes et betes, et aussi cruellement meurti grand nombre d'hommes, femmes, et enfans, et fait mourir plusieurs animaux, recordés aux informations sur ce faites, s'ensuit qu'elles sont plainement convaincues et atteintes d'etre Sorcieres. Pour reparation duquel crime a eté dit par la Cour que lesdites femmes seront presentement conduites la halte au col au lieu de supplice accoutumé, et par l'Officier criminel attachées à un poteau, pendues, etranglées, osciées, et brulées, jusqu'à ce que leur chairs et ossements soient reduits en cendres, et leurs cendres eparcées; et sont tous les biens, meubles, et heritages, si aucun en ont acquit, à Sa Majesté. Pour leur faire confesser leurs complices, qu'elles seront mises à la question en Justice avant que d'etre executées.

28

[TRANSLATION.]

Before AMICE DE CARTERET, Esq., Bailiff, and the Jurats.

JULY 4th, 1617.

SENTENCE OF DEATH.

Collette du Mont, widow of *Jean Becquet, Marie,* her daughter, wife of *Pierre Massy,* and *Isabel Becquet,* wife of *Jean Le Moygne,* being by common rumour and report for a long time past addicted to the damnable art of Witchcraft, and the same being thereupon seized and apprehended by the Officers of His Majesty [James I.], after voluntarily submitting themselves, both upon the general inquest of the country, and after having been several times brought up before the Court, heard, examined, and confronted, upon a great number of depositions made and produced before the[Pg 10] Court by the said Officers; from which it is clear and evident that for many years past the aforesaid women have practiced the diabolical art of Witchcraft, by having not only cast their spells upon inanimate objects, but also by having retained in languor through strange diseases, many persons and beasts; and also cruelly hurt a great number of men, women, and children, and caused the death of many animals, as recorded in the informations thereupon laid, it follows that they are clearly convicted and proved to be Witches. In expiation of which crime it has been ordered by the Court that the said women shall be presently conducted, with halters about their necks, to the usual place of punishment, and shall there be fastened by the Executioner to a gallows, and be hanged, strangled, killed, and burnt, until their flesh and bones are reduced to ashes, and the ashes shall be scattered; and all their goods, chattels, and estates, if any such exist, shall be forfeited to His Majesty. In order to make them disclose their accomplices, they shall be put to the question before the Court, previous to being executed.[Pg 11]

Sentence de mort ayant esté prononcée à l'encontre de *Collette Du Mont,* veuve de *Jean Becquet, Marie,* sa fille, femme de *Pierre Massy,* et *Isbel Becquet,* femme de *Jean Le Moygne,* auroyent icelles confessé comme suit:—

CONFESSION DE COLLETTE DU MONT.

Premier, la diste *Collette* immediatement appres la dyte sentence donnée, et avant que de sortir de l'auditoire, a librement recognu qu'elle estoit Sorciere; toutesfois ne voulant particularizer les crimes qu'auroit commis a esté conduite avec les autres en la Maison de la Question, et la dite question luy estant applicquée, a confessé qu'elle estoit encore jeune lors que le Diable en forme de chat: s'aparut à elle: en la Paroisse de Torteval: lors qu'elle retournoit de son bestiall, estant encore jour, et qu'il print occasion de la seduire, par l'inciter à se venger d'un de ses voisins avec lequell elle estoit pour lors en querelle pour quelque domage qu'elle auroit receu par les bestes d'yceluy; que depuis lors qu'elle avoit eu querelle avec quelcun, ill se representoit à elle en la susdite forme: et quelquefois en forme de chien: l'induisant à se venger de ceux contre lesquels elle estoit faschée: la persuadant de faire mourir des personnes et bestes.

Que le Diable l'estant venue querir pour aller au Sabat, l'appelloit sans qu'on s'en apperceust: et luy bailloit ung certain onguent noir, duquel (appres s'etre despouillée) elle se frotoit le dos, ventre et estomac: et s'estant revestuë, sortoit hors son huis, lors estoit incontinent emportée par l'air d'une grande vitesse: et se trouvoit a l'instant au lieu du Sabat, qui estoit quelquefois pres le cimetiere de la paroisse: et quelques autres fois pres le rivage de la mer, aux environs du Chateau de Rocquaine: là où estant arivée s'y rencontroit souvent quinze ou saize Sorciers et Sorcieres avec les

Diables, qu'y estoient là en forme de chiens, chats, et lievres: lesquels Sorciers et Sorcieres elle n'a peu recognoistre, parce qu'ils estoyent tous noircis et deffigurés: bien est vray avoir ouy le Diable les evocquer par leur noms, et se souvaient entre autres de la *Fallaise*, et de la *Hardie*; dit confesse qu'a l'entrée du Sabath: le Diable les voulant esvosquer commencoit par elle quelquefois. Que sa fille *Marie*, femme de *Massy*, à present condamnée pour pareill crime, est Sorciere: et qu'elle la menée par deux fois au Sabath avec elle: ne scait par où le Diable la merchée: qu'au Sabath appres avoir adoré le Diable, lequell se tenoit debout sur ses pieds de derriere, ils avoient copulation avec luy en forme de chien; puis dansoyent dos a dos. Et appres avoir dansé, beuvoyent du vin (ne scait de quelle couleur), que le Diable versoit hors d'un pot en ung gobelet d'argent ou d'estrain; lequell vin ne luy sembloit sy bon que celuy qu'on boit ordinarement; mangeoist aussy du pain blanc quj leur presentoit—n'a jamais veu de sell au Sabath.

Confesse que le Diable luy avoit donné charge d'appeler en passant *Isebell le Moygne*: lors quelle viendroit au Sabath, ce qu'elle a fait diverses fois. Qu'au partir du Sabath le Diable l'incitoit à perpetrer plusieurs maux: et pour cest effect luy bailloit certaines pouldres noires, qu'il lui commandoit de ietter sur telles personnes et bestes qu'elle voudroit; avec laquelle pouldre elle a perpetré plusieurs maux desquels ne se souvient: entres autres en ietta sur M^s *Dolbell*, ministre de la paroisse: et fut occasion de sa mort par ce moyen. Par ceste mesme pouldre ensorcela la femme de *Jean Maugues*: toutesfois nie qu'elle soit morte par son sort: qu'elle toucha par le costé, et ietta de ceste pouldre sur la femme defuncte de *Mr Perchard*, successeur ministre du dit *Dolbell*, en ycelle paroisse, ycelle estant pour lors enceinte, tellement qu'elle la fist mourir et son fruit—ne scait quelle occasion luy fut donnée par la dite femme.

Que sur le refus que la femme de *Collas Tottevin* luy fist de luy donner du laict: elle fist assecher sa vache, en iettant sur ycelle de ceste pouldre: laquelle vache elle regarit par appres en luy faisant manger du son, et de l'herbe terrestre que le Diable lui bailla.

[TRANSLATION.]

Sentence of Death having been pronounced against *Collette Du Mont*, widow of *Jean Becquet*, *Marie*, her daughter, wife of *Pierre Massy*; and *Isabel Becquet*, wife of *Jean Le Moygne*; the same have confessed as follows:—

CONFESSION OF COLLETTE DU MONT.

First, the said *Collette* immediately after the said sentence was pronounced, and before leaving the Court, freely admitted that she was a Witch; at the same time, not wishing to specify the crimes which she had committed, she was taken, along with the others, to the Torture Chamber, and the said question being applied to her, she confessed that she was quite young when the Devil, in the form of a cat: appeared to her: in the Parish of Torteval: as she was returning from her cattle, it being still daylight, and that he took occasion to lead her astray by inciting her to avenge herself on one of her neighbours, with whom she was then at enmity, on account of some damage which she had[Pg 12] suffered through the cattle of the latter; that since then when she had a quarrel with anyone, he appeared to her in the aforesaid form: and sometimes in the form of a dog: inducing her to take vengence upon those who had angered her: persuading her to cause the death of persons and cattle.

That the Devil having come to fetch her that she might go to the Sabbath, called for her without anyone perceiving it: and gave her a certain black ointment with which (after having stripped herself), she rubbed her back, belly and stomach: and then having again put on her clothes, she went out of her door, when she was immediately carried through the air at a great speed: and she found herself in an instant at the place of the Sabbath, which was sometimes near the parochial burial-ground: and at other times near the seashore in the neighbourhood of Rocquaine Castle: where, upon arrival, she met often fifteen or sixteen Wizards and Witches with the Devils who were there in the form of dogs, cats, and hares: which Wizards and Witches she was unable to recognise, because they were all blackened and[Pg 13] disfigured: it was true, however, that she had heard the Devil summon them by their names, and she remembered among others those of *Fallaise* and *Hardie*, confessed that on entering the Sabbath: the Devil wishing to summon them commenced with her sometimes. Admitted that her daughter *Marie*, wife of *Massy*, now condemned for a similar crime, was a Witch: and that she took her twice to the Sabbath with her: at the Sabbath, after having worshipped the Devil, who used to stand up on his hind legs, they had connection with him under the form of a dog; then they danced back to back. And after having danced, they drank wine (she did not know what colour it was), which the Devil poured out of a jug into a silver or pewter goblet; which wine did not seem to her so good as that which was usually drunk; they also ate white bread which he presented to them—she had never seen any salt at the Sabbath.

Confessed that the Devil had charged her to call, as she passed, for *Isabel le Moygne*: when she came to the Sabbath, which she had done several times. On leaving the Sabbath the Devil incited[Pg 14] her to commit various evil deeds: and to that effect he gave her certain black powders, which he ordered her to throw upon such persons and cattle as she wished; with this powder she perpetrated several wicked acts which she did not remember: among others she threw some upon *Mr Dolbell*, parish minister: and was the occasion of his death by these means. With this same powder she bewitched the wife of *Jean Maugues*: but denied that the woman's death was caused by it: she also touched on the side, and threw some of this powder over the deceased wife of *Mr Perchard*, the minister who succeeded the said *Dolbell* in the parish, she being *enceinte* at the time, and so caused the death of her and her infant—she did not know that the deceased woman had given her any cause for doing so.

Upon the refusal of the wife of *Collas Tottevin* to give her some milk: she caused her cow to dry up, by throwing upon it some of this powder: which cow she afterwards cured again by making it eat some bran, and some terrestrial herb that the Devil gave her.

CONFESSION DE MARIE BECQUET.

Marie, femme de *Pierre Massy*, appres sentence de mort prononcée a l'encontre d'elle, ayant esté mise a la question, a confessé qu'elle est Sorciere; et qu'à la persuation du Diable, quj s'aparut à elle en forme de chien: elle se donna à luy: que lors que se donna à luy ill la print de sa patte par la main: qu'elle s'est oint du mesme onguent que sa mere s'oignoit: et a esté au Sabath sur la banque pres du Chateau de Rocquaine, avec luy, où n'y avoit que le Diable et elle, se luy sembloit: en la susdite forme en laquelle elle la veu plusieurs fois. A été aussi au Sabath une fois entre autres en la ruë, *Collas Tottevin,* que toutes les fois qu'elle alloit au Sabath le Diable la venant querir luy sembloit qu'il la transformait en chienne; dit que sur le rivage, pres du dit Rocquaine: le Diable, en forme de chien, ayant eu copulation avec elle, luy donnoit du pain et du vin, qu'elle mangeoit et beuvoit.

Que le Diable luy bailloit certaines pouldres: lesquelles pouldres ill luy mettoit dans la main, pour ietter sur ceux qu'il luy commanderoit: qu'elle en a ietté par son commandement sur des personnes et bestes: notament sur l'enfant *Pierre Brehaut.* Item, sur la femme *Jean Bourgaize* lors qu'estoit enciente. Item, sur l'enfant *Leonard le Messurier.*

[TRANSLATION.]

CONFESSION OF MARIE BECQUET.

Marie, wife of *Pierre Massy,* after sentence of death had been pronounced against her, having been put to the question, confessed that she was a Witch; and that at the persuasion of the Devil, who appeared to her in the form of a dog: she gave herself to him: that when she gave herself to him he took her by the hand with his paw: that she used to anoint herself with the same ointment as her mother used: and had been to the Sabbath upon the bank near Rocquaine Castle with her, where there was no one but the Devil and her as it seemed: in the aforesaid form in which she had seen him several times: She was also at the Sabbath on one occasion among others in the road near *Collas Tottevin's;* every time that she went to the Sabbath, the Devil came to her, and it seemed as though he transformed her into a female dog; she said that upon the shore, near the said Rocquaine: the Devil, in the form of a dog, having had connection with her, gave her bread and wine, which she ate and drank.

The Devil gave her certain powders: which powders he put into her hand, for her to throw upon those whom he ordered her: she threw some of them by his orders upon persons and cattle: notably upon the child of *Pierre Brehaut.* Item, upon the wife of *Jean Bourgaize,* while she was *enceinte.* Item, upon the child of *Leonard le Messurier.*

CONFESSION D'ISABEL BECQUET.

Isebelle, femme de *Jean de Moygne*, ayant esté mise a la question, a tout aussytost confessé qu'elle est Sorciere: et que sur ce qu'elle tomba en querelle avec la *Girarde*, sa belle-s[oe]ur: le Diable en forme de lievre print occasion de la seduire: se representant à elle en plain jour dans une ruë pres de sa maison: et la persuadant et incitant de se donner à luy: et que l'aideroit à se venger de la dite *Girarde* et de tous aultres: à laquelle persuasion n'ayant icelle à l'instant voulu condescendre: aussy tout disparut: mais incontinent luy vint derechef au devant en la mesme ruë, et poursuyvant sa premiere pointe: l'exhortoit aux mesmes fins que dessus: cela fait, ill la laissa et se retira, apres luy avoir, au prealable, mis une pochée de pasnés; qu'elle portoit pour lors, une certaine pouldre noire envelopée dans ung linge qu'il mist: laquelle pouldre elle retint par devers soy. S'aparut à elle une autre fois en mesme forme au territoire de la ville, l'incitant derechef à se donner à luy, à quoy ne voulant icelle condescendre luy fist adonc requeste de luy donner une beste vive: lors de ce pas revint ches elle querir ung poullet, qu'elle luy apporta au mesme lieu où l'avoit laissé, lequell ill print: et appres l'avoir remerecie luy donna assignation de se trouver le lendemain avant jour au Sabath, avec promesse qu'il l'enverroit querir: suivant laquelle promesse, estant la nuittée ensuivant, la vielle *Collette du Mont* venant la querir, lui bailla de l'onguent noir qu'elle avoit eu du Diable; duquell (après s'estre despouillée) s'oignit le dos, et le ventre, puis s'estant revestuë, sortit l'huis de sa maison: lors fut à l'instant enlevée: et transportée au travers hayes et buissons, pres la banque sur le bord de la mer, aux environs du Chasteau de Rocquaine, lieu ordinaire où le Diable gardoit son Sabath; là où ne fut sytost arivée, que le Diable ne vint la trouver en forme de chien avec deux grandes cornes dressées en hault: et de l'une de ses pattes (qui lui sembloyent comme mains), la print par la main: et l'appellant par son nom, luy dist qu'estoit la bien venuë: lors aussytost le Diable la fist mettre sur ses genoux: luy se tenant debout sur ses pieds de derrière; luy ayant fait detester l'Esternelle en ses mots: *Je renie Dieu le Pere, Dieu le Fils et Dieu le St. Esprit*, se fist adorer et invocquer en ses termes: *Nostre Grand Maistre aide nous!* avec paction expresse d'adherer à luy; que cela fait, ill ont copulation avec elle en la susdite forme de chien, ung peu plus grand: puis elle et les aultres danserent avec luy dos à dos: qu'apres avoir dansé, le Diable versoit hors d'un pot du vin noir, qu'il leur presentoit dans une escuelle de bois, duquell elle beut, toutesfois ne luy sembloit sy bon que le vin quj se boit ordinairement: qu'il y avoit du pain—mais n'en mangea point: confesse qu'elle se donna lors à luy pour ung mois: ainsy retournerent du Sabath comme y estoyent allés.

Que seconde fois fut au Sabath, apres que la vielle *Collette* l'eut esté querir et qu'elle se fist oindre d'onguent cy dessus;— declare qu'à l'entree du Sabath eut dereschef copulation avec le Diable, et dansa avec luy; appres avoir dansé, à sa solicitation de prolonger le temps, se donna à luy pour trois ans; qu'au Sabath le Diable faisoit evocation des Sorciers et Sorcieres par ordre (se souvient tresbien y avoir ouy le Diable appeller la vielle *Collette*, la premiere, en ces termes: *Madame la Vielle Becquette*); puis la *Fallaise*, appres la *Hardie*. Item, *Marie*, femme de *Massy*, fille de la dite *Collette*. Dit appres eux, elle mesme estoit evosquée par le Diable, en ses termes: *La Petite Becquette*; qu'elle y a ouy aussy evosquer *Collas Becquet*, fils de la dit vielle (lequell la tenoit par la main en dansant, et une que ne cognoist la tenoit par l'autre main): qu'il y en avoit viron six autres que ne cognoissoit: que la dite vielle estoit tousjours proche du Diable: que quelque fois tandis que les uns dansoyent les autres avoyent copulation avec les Diables en forme de chien: et estoyent au Sabath viron trois ou quatre heures, non plus.

Qu'estant au Sabath le Diable la mercha en haut de la cuisse: laquelle merche ayant esté reuisitée par les sage femmes, ont raporté avoir mis dedans une petite espingue bien avant, qu'elle n'a point senty, et n'en est sorty aulcuns sang; ne scait par ou le Diable a merche les autres: que les premiers venues au lieu du Sabath attendoyent les autres; et apparoissoyent tous les Sorciers et Sorcieres en leur propre formes: toutesfois noircis et defficgurés, et ne les pouvoit en cognoistre.

Que le Diable apparoissoit quelque fois en forme de boucq au Sabath; ne la veu en autres formes; qu'au departir, ill se faisoit baiser la derriere, leur demandant quant reviendroyent: les exhortoit qu'eussent à adherer tousiours a luy: et faire des maux, et pour cest effet leur bailloit certaines pouldres noires envelopées dans ung drapeau, pour en ietter sur ceux qu'ils vouloyent ensorcerer: qu'au departir du Sabath le Diable s'en alloit d'un coste et eux de l'autre: appres les avoir toutes prinses par la main: Qu'à l'instigation du Diable elle en a jetté sur plusieurs personnes et bestes: notament sur *Jean Jehan*, lors qu'il vint chez elle querir ung pourceau. Item, sur l'enfant *James Gallienne*, et sur aultres: Item, sur les bestes de *Brouart* et aultres.

Que c'estoit le Diable qui fut veu ches le susdit *Gallienne*, en forme de rat et bellette, ycelle estant pour lors aux environs de la maison du dit *Gallienne*, et s'estant venu rendre à elle en resemblance d'homme, la frapa de plusieurs coups par le visage et teste: dont estoit ainsy meurdie et deschirée lors que fut veüe le lendemain par *Thomas Sohier*. Et croit que la cause de ce maltraitement fut pour ce que ne voulut aller avec le Diable chez le dit *Gallienne*.

Qu'elle n'alloit point au Sabath sinon lors que son mary estoit demeuré la nuict en pescherie à la mer.

Que lors qu'elle vouloit ensorceler quelcun, sa poudre estant faillie, le Diable s'aparoissoit à elle, luy disant qu'allast en querir en tell endroit qu'il luy nommoit, ce qu'elle faisoit, et ne falloit d'y en trouver.

[TRANSLATION.]

CONFESSION OF ISABEL BECQUET.

Isabel, wife of *Jean le Moygne,* having been put to the question, at once confessed that she was a Witch: and that upon her getting into a quarrel with the woman *Girarde,* who was her sister-in-law: the Devil, in the form of a hare, took occasion to tempt her: appearing to her in broad daylight in a road near her house: and persuading and inciting her to give herself to him: and that he would help her to avenge herself on the said *Girarde,* and everybody else: to which persuasion she would not at the moment condescend to yield: so he at once disappeared: but very soon he came again to her in the same road, and pursuing his previous argument: exhorted her in the same terms as above: that done, he left her and went away, after having previously put her a[Pg 17] sackful of parsnips; she then took a certain black powder wrapped in a cloth which he placed; which powder she kept by her. He appeared to her another time under the same form in the town district, inciting her anew to give herself to him, but she not wishing to comply, he next made a request to her to give him some living animal: whereupon she returned to her dwelling and fetched a chicken, which she carried to him to the same place where she had left him, and he took it: and after having thanked her he made an appointment for her to be present the next morning before daylight at the Sabbath, promising that he would send for her: according to which promise, during the ensuing night, the old woman *Collette du Mont,* came to fetch her, and gave her some black ointment, which she had had from the Devil; with this (after having stripped herself) she anointed her back and belly, then having dressed herself again she went out of her house door: when she was instantly caught

39

up: and carried across hedges and bushes to the bank on the sea shore, in the neighbourhood of Rocquaine Castle, the usual place where the Devil kept his Sabbath; no sooner had she arrived there than the[Pg 18] Devil came to her in the form of a dog, with two great horns sticking up: and with one of his paws (which seemed to her like hands) took her by the hand: and calling her by her name told her that she was welcome: then immediately the Devil made her kneel down: while he himself stood up on his hind legs; he then made her express detestation of the Eternal in these words: *I renounce God the Father, God the Son, and God the Holy Ghost*, and then caused her to worship and invoke himself in these terms: *Our Great Master, help us!* with a special compact to be faithful to him; and when this was done he had connection with her in the aforesaid form of a dog, but a little larger: then she and the others danced with him back to back: after having danced, the Devil poured out of a jug some black wine, which he presented to them in a wooden bowl, from which she drank, but it did not seem to her so good as the wine which is usually drunk: there was also bread—but she did not eat any: confessed that she gave herself to him for a month: they returned from the Sabbath in the same manner that they went there.

The second time she was at the Sabbath was after the old[Pg 19] woman *Collette* had been to fetch her, and she anointed herself with the ointment as above stated;—declared, that on entering the Sabbath, she again had connection with the Devil and danced with him; after having danced, and upon his solicitation to prolong the time, she gave herself to him for three years; at the Sabbath the Devil used to summon the Wizards and Witches in regular order (she remembered very well having heard him call the old woman *Collette* the first, in these terms: *Madame the Old Woman Becquette*): then the woman *Fallaise*; and afterwards the woman *Hardie*. Item, he also called *Marie*, wife of *Massy*, and daughter of the said *Collette*. Said that after them, she herself was called

40

by the Devil: in these terms: *The Little Becquettc*: she also heard him call there *Collas Becquet*, son of the said old woman (who [*Collas*] held her by the hand in dancing, and someone [a woman] whom she did not know, held her by the other hand): there were about six others there she did not know: the said old woman was always the nearest to the Devil: occasionally while some were dancing, others were having connection with the Devils in the form of dogs; they remained at the Sabbath about three or four hours, not more.[Pg 20]

While at the Sabbath the Devil marked her at the upper part of the thigh: which mark having been examined by the midwives, they reported that they had stuck a small pin deeply into it, and that she had not felt it, and that no blood had issued: she did not know in what part the Devil had marked the others: those who came first to the place of the Sabbath, waited for the others; and all the Wizards and Witches appeared in their proper forms: but blackened and disfigured so that they could not be recognised.

The Devil appeared sometimes in the form of a goat at the Sabbath; never saw him in other forms: on their departure he made them kiss him behind, and asked them when they would come again: he exhorted them always to be true to him: and to do evil deeds, and to this end he gave them certain black powders, wrapped in a cloth, for them to throw upon those whom they wished to bewitch: on leaving the Sabbath, the Devil went away in one direction and they in the other: after he had taken them all by the hand: At the instigation of the Devil she threw some of the powder over several persons and cattle: notably over *Jean*[Pg 21] *Jehan*, when he came to her house to look for a pig. Item, over the child of *James Gallienne*, and over others. Item, over the cattle of *Brouart*, and of others.

It was the Devil that was seen at the said *Gallienne's* house in the form of a rat and a weazle, she herself being then in the neighbourhood of *Gallienne's* house, and he [the Devil] came to her in the form of a man, and struck her several blows on the face and head: by which she was bruised and torn in the way that she was seen the next day by *Thomas Sohier.* And she believed that the cause of this maltreatment was because she would not go with the Devil to the house of the said *Gallienne.*

She never went to the Sabbath except when her husband remained all night fishing at sea.

Whenever she wanted to bewitch anyone and her powder happened to have been all used up, the Devil appeared to her and told her to go to such a place, which he named, for some more, and when she did so, she never failed to find it there.

DEPOSITIONS CONTRE COLLAS BECQUET.

Le xvij Mai 1617.

Susanne Le Tellier, veufve de *Pierre Rougier,* depose que son mary estant decedé, trouva des sorcerots en son lict; et qu'en son djt lict mortuaire, il se plaignoit esté ensorcelé par *Collas Becquet,* avec lequel avoit eu dispute, sur laquelle dispute luy dyt que s'en repentiroit; et la dessus fut prins de m... duquel fut douze jours malade; qu'ils trouverent quarante-quatre sorcerots en l'oreiller de son enfant, que les uns estoyent fait comme herissons, les autres comme pommes, et les autres plats comme la rouelle de la main; et du fill de chanvre entortillé avec de plumes.

Susanne, femme de *Jean Le Messurier*, depose que son mary et *Collas Becquet* plaiderent à jour passé ensemble; qu'allors ils avoyent ung enfant ayant de viron six semaines, et comme elle le despouilloit au soir, pour le coucher, il tomba sur l'estomac du djt enfant une beste noire laquelle fondit si tost que fut tombée, d'aultant qu'elle fist debvoir de la rechercher et ne peut jamais apercevoir qu'elle devint; incontinent l'enfant fut prins de mal et ne voulu teter, mais fut fort tormenté; que s'estant avisée de regarder dans l'oreiller du djt enfant y trouverent des sorcerots cousus de fil, et les ayant tirés et bien espluché la plume de l'oreiller, y regarda sept jours appres et y entrouva derechef avec une febve noire percée; dequoy, ayant le djt *Becquet* ouy qu'il en estoit suspecté, sa femme vint ches la deposante comme le djt *Becquet* estoit à la mer, et luy djt qu'à raison du bruit que la deposante avoit sucité sur son mary, iceluy *Becquet* fuetteroit le djt *Mesurier*, son mary, et elle, et les tueroit; qu'apres cela la deposante fut ches eux leur dire que ne les craignoit, ny luy ny elle, de ce qu'ils la menacoyent de tuer son mary et elle; qu'ayant la deposante un jour six grands poulets qui couroyent appres leur mere, ils sortirent de leur maison et revinent au soir; et un à un se mirent a saulter en hault contre la cheminée et manget la scie, qu'ils moururent tous un à un, à voy ... comme ils sautoyent, jusques au dernier qui dura en vie jusqu'à une heure devant le jour qu'il mourut; que depuis que l'eurent declare à Mr *Deljsle* et les eut menacés, il a amendé à son enfant et se porte bien.

Collas Rougier depose que son frere *Piere Rougier* en mourant chargeoit *Collas Becquet* de sa mort.

Collas Hugues raport qu'estant en une nopsce y survint *Collas Becquet* jouet avec sa belle-fille, laquelle le rebouta; et des le mesme soir elle fut frapée de telle facon qu'on pensoit qu'elle mourust à chacune heure; qu'elle est demeurée mechaignée de coste, et trouva un des sorcerots en son lict, qui pour lors furent monstrés à Messrs de Justice qui estoyent à tenir des veues à St. Pierre; que la djte fille tomboit quelque fois y terre toute aveuglée.

La femme du djt *Hugues* depose tout de mesme que son mary.

Jean De Garis, fils *Guillaume*, depose qu'il y a viron deux ou trois ans qu'ayant presté quelque argent sur un gage à *Collas Becquet*, luy demandant son argent, ou qu'il feroit ventiller son gage; luy repartit le djt *Becquet* à feray donc ventiller autre chose; qu'estant le djt *de Garis* arivé en sa maison, trouva la fille malade et affligée; qu'ils trouverent des sorcerots et aultres brouilleries par plusieurs fois à l'oreiller de leur enfant; mais que la mere du djt *Becquet* estant venue en la maison du djt *de Garis*, luy donna à boire de l'eau et la moitié d'un pain comme avoit esté conseillé de faire; depuis ne trouverent plus rien à l'oreiller du djt enfant; toutesfois pour eviter les djts sorcerots, ont toujours depuis couché leur enfant sur la paille; croit que ce mal leur ariva par leur moyen.

Mr Thomas de Ljsle depose que *Thomas Brouart*, qui demeure en sa maison, ayant appellé le fils de *Collas Becquet*, sorcier, il arriva qu'il fut un jour trouvé au lict du djt *Thomas* grand nombre de vers, et les ayant le djt *Sieur de Ljsle* veus, les jugea comme une formioniere, tant estoyent mouvans et espais, et à peine en peuvent vuider le dit enfant, l'ayant mis en plusieurs endroits; qu'appres fut le djt enfant accueillis de poulx de telle maniere que quoyque luy changeassent des chemises et habits tous les jours ne l'en pouvoyent franchir; et qu'ayant le djt *Thomas Brouart* un corset tout neuf, fut tellement couvert de poulx qu'on n'auroit peu cognoistre le drap, et fut contraint le faire jetter parmy les choux; surquoy fait menacer aultre *Massi* de la batre si elle ne s'abstenoit d'ainsy traiter son enfant; qu'estant revenu trouva le djt corset parmis les choux denue de poulx, lesquels du depuis ont quitté le djt *Brouart*.

Jacques le Mesurier depose qu'il y a viron deux ou trois ans qu'il rencontra *Collas Becquet* et *Perot Massi*, quj avoyent du poisson, et d'aultant qu'ils lui debvoyent de l'argent, il voulut prendre de leur poisson à rabatre, mais ne luy en voulant bailler, eurent quelque dispute; sur quoy l'un des djts *Becquet* ou *Massi* le menacerent qu'il s'en repentiroit; qu'au bout de deux ou trois jours il fut saisi d'un mal que le brusloit, et quelques fois devenoit tout morfondu, sans qu'on le peust eschauffer, et sans aulcune relache; qu'il fut en ces tourments pres d'un mois. *Collas Becquet* entendit que le deposant le chargeoit d'estre causte de son mal, et menacoit qu'il tueroit le djt deposant; mais bientost appres fut le djt deposant guery; dit de cuider et de croire les djts *Becquet* et *Massy*, ou un d'iceux, fut cause de son mal.

[TRANSLATION.]

DEPOSITIONS AGAINST COLLAS BECQUET.

MAY 17, 1617.

Susanne Le Tellier, widow of *Pierre Rougier*, deposed that after her husband was dead she found witches' spells in his bed; and that while he was upon his said deathbed he complained of being bewitched by *Collas Becquet*, with whom he had had a quarrel, and who during the quarrel told him he would repent of it; whereupon he was taken with ...', whereof he was ill for twelve days; they also found forty-four witches' spells in her child's pillow, some of which were made like hedgehogs, others round like apples, and others again flat like the palm of the hand; and they were of hempen thread twisted with feathers.

Susanne, wife of *Jean Le Messurier*, deposed that her husband and *Collas Becquet* had angry words together one day; they had an infant about six weeks old, and as she was undressing it in the evening to put it to bed, there fell upon the stomach of the said[Pg 23] infant, a black beast which melted away as soon as it fell, so that although she carefully sought for it, she could never discover what had become of it; immediately afterwards the infant was taken ill and would not suck, but was much tormented; being advised to look into the said infant's pillow, she found there several witches' spells sewn with thread; these she took out and carefully dressed all the feathers in the pillow; yet when she examined it again a week afterwards, she found there a black bean with a hole in it; of which, the said *Becquet* hearing that he was suspected, his wife came to witness's house while the said *Becquet* was at sea, and told her that on account of the rumour which witness had raised about her husband, he the said *Becquet* would thrash the said *Messurier*, her husband, and herself, and would kill them; after that, witness went to their house to say they were not afraid either of him or her, or of their threats to kill her husband and her; witness had six big chickens which ran after their mother, going out of the house in the morning and returning at night; and one by one they began to jump up against the chimney and eat the soot, so that they all died one after the other, ... as they jumped, until the last one which remained alive up to one hour of daybreak, when it died; after they had told this to *Mr. de Lisle*, and he had threatened the people, her infant recovered and remained well.

Collas Rougier deposed that his brother *Pierre Rougier* when dying charged *Collas Becquet* with causing his death.

Collas Hugues reported that being at a wedding, *Collas Becquet* arrived there, and began to toy with his daughter-in-law, who repelled his advances; the very same evening she was taken ill in such a manner that they thought she would have died from one hour to another; besides which she remained under the charm, and they found one of the witches' spells in her bed, which was shown to the Members of the Court, who were making an inspection at St. Peter's; the said girl sometimes fell to the ground quite blinded.

The wife of the said *Hugues* deposed to exactly the same as her husband.

Jean de Garis, son of *William*, deposed that about two or three years ago, having lent some money on pledge to *Collas Becquet*, he asked him for the money, or else for a verification of his security;[Pg 25] when the said *Becquet* replied that he would let him know what his security was; the said *de Garis* having then returned home, found his daughter sick and afflicted; they found witches' spells and other conjurations several times in their child's pillow; but the mother of the said *Becquet* having come to the said *de Garis's* house, he gave her a drink of water and half-a-loaf of bread, as he had been advised to do; since which time they had found nothing more in the child's pillow; however to avoid all risk of the said witches' spells they had always since then let their child sleep upon straw; he fully believed that this evil had come upon them by their means.

Mr. Thomas de Lisle deposed that *Thomas Brouart*, who resided in his house, having called the son of *Collas Becquet* a wizard, it happened that there was one day found in the said *Thomas's* bed a great number of maggots, which the said *Sieur de Lisle* saw, and compared to an ant-hill, so lively and thick were they, and they could hardly clear the said child of them, although they put it in different places; afterwards the said child gathered lice in such a manner that although its shirts and clothes were[Pg 26] changed every day they could not free it; the said *Thomas Brouart* also had a brand new vest, which was so covered with lice that it was impossible to see the cloth, and he was compelled to have it thrown among the cabbages; upon which he went and threatened *Massi's* wife that he would beat her if she did not abstain from thus treating his child; and on returning he found the said vest among the cabbages clear of lice, which had also since then quitted the said *Brouart*.

Jacques le Mesurier deposed that about two or three years ago he met *Collas Becquet* and *Perot Massi*, who had some fish and who moreover owed him money; he wished to take some of their fish at a reduced price, but they would not agree to it, and they quarrelled; whereupon one of the two, either *Becquet* or *Massi*, threatened him that he would repent of it; and at the end of two or three days, he was seized with a sickness in which he first burnt like fire and then was benumbed with cold so that nothing would warm him, and this without any cessation; he suffered in this way for nearly a month. *Collas Becquet* heard that witness charged him with being the cause of his sickness, and he threatened that he would[Pg 27] kill witness; but very soon afterwards the said witness was cured; and he affirms and believes that the said *Becquet* and *Massy*, or one of them, was the cause of his attack.

NOTE ON THE GUERNSEY RECORDS.

The Records at the Guernsey *Greffe*, from which the foregoing confessions and depositions have been transcribed, and whence the following list of accusations is compiled, are of a very voluminous character. In fact there is enough matter in them, connected with Witchcraft alone, to fill at least a couple of thick octavo volumes. There is, however, so much sameness in the different cases, and such a common tradition running through the whole, that the present excerpts give a very fair idea of the features which characterise the mass. While some of these Records are tolerably complete, the greater part of them unfortunately are fragmentary and imperfect. The books in which they were originally written seem to have been formed of a few sheets of paper stitched together. Then at some later period a number of these separate sections—in a more or less tattered condition—were gathered into volumes and bound together in vellum. It is evident, however, that very little care was exercised in their arrangement in chronological order. The consequence is that one portion of a trial sometimes occurs in one part of a volume, and the rest in another part; sometimes the depositions alone seem to have been preserved; sometimes the confessions; while in many cases the sentences pronounced are all that can now be discovered. Nevertheless these old Records enshrine much that is interesting, and very well deserve a more exhaustive analysis than they have ever yet received. There are also in the margins of these volumes, scores of pen-and-ink sketches of a most primitive description, depicting the carrying out of the various rigours of the law. Rough and uncouth as these illustrations are, they nevertheless possess a good deal of graphic significance, and I hope to reproduce some of them in facsimile, in a future publication. They represent, for instance, culprits hanging on the gallows—sometimes two or three in a row—with a fire kindled underneath; others attached to stakes in the midst of the flames; others, again, racing away under the lash of the executioner, &c., &c., and thus form a most realistic comment on the judicial severities recorded in the text.

WITCHCRAFT TRIALS IN GUERNSEY,

From 1563 to 1634, a period of 71 years.

QUEEN ELIZABETH.—1558-1603.

HELIER GOSSELIN, Bailiff, 1550-1563.

November 19th, 1563.

Gracyene Gousset,
Catherine Prays,
Collette Salmon, wife of Collas Dupont,

Condemned to death and the Royal pardon refused.

December 17th, 1563.

Françoise Regnouff,
Martin Tulouff,

Condemned to death and the Royal pardon refused.

December 22nd, 1563.

Collette Gascoing.

This woman was found guilty, and the Royal pardon being refused, she was whipped, had one of her ears cut off, and was banished from the island.

THOMAS COMPTON, Bailiff, 1563-1572.

July 30th, 1570.

Jeannette Du Mareesc,

Was banished for seven years.

October 27th, 1570.

Michelle Tourtell,

Banished from the island.

November 3rd, 1570.

Coliche Tourtell,
James de la Rue,

Both banished from the island.

November 10th, 1570.

Lorenche Faleze, wife of Henry Johan,

Banished from the island.

November 17th, 1570.

Thomasse Salmon.
Marie Gauvein, wife of Ozouet.

Both these women were whipped, had each an ear cut off, and were banished from the island.

GUILLAUME BEAUVOIR, Bailiff, 1572-1581.

No prosecutions for Witchcraft seem to have taken place during his tenure of office.

THOMAS WIGMORE, Bailiff, 1581-1588.

1583.

Collas de la Rue.

The result of this trial is uncertain.

LOUIS DEVYCKE, Bailiff, 1588-1600.

No Witchcraft prosecutions during his term of office.

KING JAMES I.—1603-1625.

AMICE DE CARTERET, Bailiff, 1601-1631.

1611.

Marie Rolland.

The result of this trial is uncertain.

June 11th, 1613.

Oliver Omont,
Cecille Vaultier, wife of Omont,
Guillemine, their daughter,

Were all banished from the island.

July 17th, 1613.

Laurence Leustace, wife of Thomas Le Compte,

Banished from the island.

July 4th, 1617.

Collette du Mont, widow of Jean Becquet.
Marie, her daughter, wife of Pierre Massy.
Isabel Becquet, wife of Jean Le Moygne.

All three women, after being found guilty, confessed under torture, and were then hanged and burnt.

August 8th, 1617.

Michelle Jervaise, widow Salmon.
Jeanne Guignon, wife of J. de Callais, and two of her children.

These four persons were hanged and burnt, after being put to the question.

October 17th, 1617.

Marie de Callais.
Philipine le Parmentier, widow of Nicolle, of Sark.

These two women were hanged and burnt, after being previously put to the question.

[Pg 30]

November 25th, 1617.

Thomasse de Calais, wife of Isaac le Patourel,

Banished from the island.

November 25th, 1617.

Christine Hamon, wife of Etienne Gobetell.

This woman was banished from the island, but returned on May 6th, 1626, when she was again arrested and sentenced to death. She was hanged July 21st, 1626.

August 1st, 1618.

Jean de Callais, together with his son, and servants.

All these were charged with practicing Witchcraft, and were sent out of the island.

53

December, 1618.

Jean Nicolle, of Sark,

Being found guilty, was whipped, had an ear cut off, and was banished from the island.

May 1st, 1619.

Pierre Massi,

Condemned to be hanged. He, however, contrived to get out of prison and drowned himself.

August 7th, 1619.

Jeanne Behot,

Banished from the island.

April 22nd, 1620.

Girete Parmentier,
Jeanne Le Cornu, widow of Collas le Vallois.

These two women were banished.

May 8th, 1622.

Collette de l'Estac, wife of Thomas Tourgis.
Collette Robin.
Catherine Hallouris, widow Heaulme.

These three women were hanged and burnt, after being put to the question.

October 17th, 1622.

Thomas Tourgis, of the Forest.
Jeanne Tourgis, his daughter.
Michelle Chivret, wife of Pierre Omont.

All three were burnt alive.

October 19th, 1622.

Jean Le Moigne.
Guillemine la Bousse.

This man and woman were set at liberty.

November 30th, 1622.

Perine Marest, wife of Pierre Gauvin,

Banished, together with her husband and children.

[Pg 31]

October 3rd, 1623.

Etienne Le Compte,

Hanged and burnt.

May 28th, 1624.

Marguerite Tardif, wife of P. Ozanne,

Set at liberty.

June 4th, 1624.

Ester Henry, wife of Jean de France.

This woman was burnt alive. The sentence states that her flesh and bones are to be reduced to ashes and scattered by the winds, as being unworthy of any sepulture.

July 16th, 1624.

Collette la Gelée.

This woman was hanged and burnt.

October 22nd, 1624.

Jean Quaripel,

Hanged and burnt.

KING CHARLES I.—1625-1649.

July 23rd, 1625.

Elizabeth, wife of Pierre Duquemin,

Banished for 7 years.

August 11th, 1626.

Jeanne de Bertran, wife of Jean Thomas,

Hanged and burnt.

August 12th, 1626.

Marie Sohier, wife of J. de Garis,

Hanged and burnt.

November 10th, 1626.

Judith Alexander, of Jersey, wife of Pierre Jehan,

Hanged and burnt.

August 25th, 1627.

Job Nicolle, of Sark,

Condemned to perpetual banishment.

January 16th, 1629.

Anne Blampied, wife of Thomas Heaulme, of the Forest.
Thomas Heaulme, of the Forest.

Both banished for seven years.

May 1st, 1629.

Marguerite Picot (l'Aubaine),

Hanged and burnt.

August 7th, 1629.

Susanne Prudhome, wife of Guilbert, of the Castel,

Put to the question, hanged, and burnt.

[Pg 32]

JEAN DE QUETTEVILLE, Bailiff, 1631-1644.

July 1st, 1631.

Jehan Nicolle, of Sark,

Set at liberty.

July 15th, 1631.

Marie Mabile, wife of Pierre de Vauriouf.
Thomas Civret.

Both were put to the question, hanged, and burnt.

July 23rd, 1631.

Susanne Rouane, wife of Etienne Le Compte,
Judith Le Compte, }
Bertrane   "   } four daughters of the above.
Ester   "   }
Rachel   "   }

The mother was condemned to perpetual banishment from the island, and the daughters were banished for fifteen years.

October 1st, 1631.

Marie Mortimer, wife of François Chirret.
Also her son.

Both were set at liberty.

October 1st, 1631.

Vincente Canu, wife of André Odouère.
Marie de Callais.

Both were set at liberty.

December 10th, 1631.

Jehan Canivet.
Renette de Garis, wife of Martin Maugeur.
Elizabeth le Hardy, wife of Collas Deslandes.
Simeone Mollett.
Marie Clouet, wife of Pierre Beneste.

All the above were condemned to perpetual banishment.

January 28th, 1634.

Jacob Gaudion, of Alderney,

Condemned to perpetual banishment.

May 16th, 1634.

Marie Guillemotte, wife of Samuel Roland, known as Dugorne.
Marie Rolland, her daughter.

The mother was hanged and burnt, and the daughter was condemned to perpetual banishment.

THE STORY IN BRIEF

OF THE

GUILLE-ALLÈS LIBRARY,

GUERNSEY.

BY J. LINWOOD PITTS.

In concluding the editorial duties connected with the issue of this fourth volume of the "Guille-Allès Library Series," it seems to me that the time is an opportune one for adding some short account of the origin and foundation of the noble Institution from which the "Series" takes its name. The Guille-Allès Library is proving such an immense boon to our little insular community, that very naturally, many inquiries are from time to time made—especially by strangers—as to how its existence came about.

In order to answer these questions we must go as far back as the year 1834. At that time Mr. Guille—who is a Guernseyman by birth—was but a boy of sixteen, and had been two years in America. He was serving his apprenticeship with a well-known firm in New York, and he enjoyed the privilege of access to a very extensive library in that city, founded by a wealthy corporation known as *The General Society of Mechanics and Tradesmen*. The pleasure and profit which he derived from this source were so great, and made such a deep impression upon his mind that, young as he was, he formed the resolution that if his future life proved prosperous, and his position enabled him to do so, he would one day found a similar institution in his own little native island of Guernsey. Throughout the whole of his future career this intention was present with him; and commencing at once,—in spite of his then very limited means—to purchase books which should form a[Pg 34] nucleus for the anticipated collection, he began to lay the foundation of the literary treasures which crowd the shelves of the Guille-Allès Library to-day. At the age of twenty, when out of his apprenticeship, he found himself the possessor of several hundreds of volumes of standard works, many of which are now in the Library, and upon which he must naturally look with peculiar and very legitimate pleasure, as being the corner stones of the subsequent splendid superstructure.

Business affairs prospered with Mr. Guille. As time rolled on he was taken into partnership with the firm, as was also his friend and fellow-countryman, Mr. F.M. Allès, and his increasing prosperity enabled him to put his cherished project into more tangible shape. While on a visit to Guernsey in 1851, he wrote a few articles in the *Gazette Officielle*, with the view of drawing public attention to the importance of forming district or parish libraries. These articles attracted the notice of *The Farmers' Club*, an association of intelligent country gentlemen who met at the Castel. Their secretary, the late Mr. Nicholas Le Beir, wrote to Mr. Guille at the request of the members, informing him of their appreciation of his views, and of his having been elected an honorary member of their association, in token of their esteem. They had previously elected in a similar way the famous French poet Béranger, and also Guernsey's national bard, the late Mr. George Métivier. Mr. Guille accepted the honour, and the correspondence which ensued resulted in his offering his collection of books—supplemented by a considerable sum of money—towards forming the commencement of such libraries as he had been advocating. Nothing, however, really definite was done until Mr. Guille's next visit to Guernsey in 1855-6, when after consultation with that devoted friend of education, the late Mr. Peter Roussel, a meeting of a few friends—including Mr. Roussel and his venerable mother, Mr. Guille, Judge Clucas,

Mr. Le Beir, and Mr. Henry E. Marquand—who were known to be favourable to the project was held, several handsome subscriptions were promised, Mr. Guille renewed his offer previously made[Pg 35] to *The Farmers' Club*, and a workable scheme was matured.

THE GUILLE LIBRARY,

for so the Committee decided to name the undertaking, consequently commenced its useful career in 1856. The collection of books was divided into five sections, which were placed in separate cases, and located at convenient distances about the island—where they were taken charge of by friends—the largest being reserved for the town. The intention was to exchange these cases in rotation, and so establish a circulating library in the most comprehensive sense of the term. But this was, in reality, never carried out, for after the volumes had been read in their respective stations, they were returned to their places, and left to slumber unused, until Mr. Guille once more came to the island in 1867, with the intention of remaining permanently, and he then had them all brought to town and arranged in one central *depôt.*

Mr. Guille also opened a branch Reading-room and Library at St. Martin's, in the hope of being able thereby to draw the young men of the parish from the degrading attractions of the public house. For three years he kept this comfortable room open, while in winter and summer neither rain nor storm prevented him from being present there every evening to personally superintend the undertaking. Ultimately, however, he found the strain too much for his health, and he discontinued the branch so as to concentrate more attention upon the central establishment in town.

For five-and-twenty years, from 1856 to 1881, Mr. Guille worked steadily and unostentatiously at the benevolent enterprise which he had inaugurated. Death removed several of his early coadjutors, and for many years he bore all the financial burdens and toiled on single-handed and alone. What was still more discouraging was that he unfortunately had to encounter for a very long time an almost incredible amount of mental supineness on the part of those whom he was so disinterestedly seeking to benefit. It was not as though[Pg 36] any desire for knowledge existed among the mass of the Guernsey people, and he only had to assume the pleasant duty of satisfying that desire. Such a desire did not exist. Many of the people not only never had read any books but they flatly declined to begin. Mr. Guille felt that this deplorable attitude ought to be combatted, and he therefore persevered in the thankless and difficult task of trying in the first place to create the want, and in the second place to satisfy it. A quarter-of-a-century's earnest effort in a good cause, however, cannot fail to produce some fruit, and within the last three or four years much brighter days have dawned. Mr. Guille's lifelong friend and former business partner, Mr. F.M. Allès,—who had often previously substantially assisted him,—has latterly thoroughly associated himself with the work, and the result is that the rudimentary scheme of 1856 has at length culminated in the splendid

GUILLE-ALLÈS LIBRARY,

which was thrown open to the public in the old Assembly Rooms, on the 2nd of January, 1882, and bears on its portal the appropriate motto: *Ingredere ut proficias*—"Enter that thou mayst profit." How admirably this fine Institution is fulfilling its mission is well-known to all who frequent it. It already contains a collection of over 35,000 volumes—to which constant additions are being made—of valuable and standard works in all branches of science, literature and art, both in the French and English languages, besides numerous works in German, Italian, Greek, Latin, &c. It has a commodious Reading-room, well supplied with journals and periodical publications; while a Society of Natural Science has also been inaugurated and meets in connection with it. The Guernsey Mechanics' Institution—after an existence of just half-a-century—was absorbed into it at the close of 1881; and the Library of the *Société Guernesiaise*—founded in 1867—now finds a home on its shelves. The subscription for membership is merely nominal, and Messrs. Guille and Allès have made arrangements to endow the Institution[Pg 37] with such ample funds as shall secure in perpetuity the many benefits which it is conferring upon the island.

THE FUTURE OF THE INSTITUTION

is therefore fully assured and its wants provided for. The spacious new buildings which have been for many months in process of erection are now (December, 1885) rapidly approaching completion. They comprise a spacious and handsome Lecture Hall, capable of seating from 250 to 300 persons; a Book-room 63-ft. by 25-ft., exclusively for the lending department, and which will accommodate on its shelves from 45,000 to 50,000 additional volumes—with a large anteroom for the convenience of the subscribers. The present Reading-room will then be used for a Reference Library and Students' Consulting and Reading-room. There are also a General Reading-room, a Working Men's Reading-room, and numerous apartments suitable for Class-rooms and Committee-rooms. The roof of the original building has been reconstructed and raised so as to form a suite of rooms 100-ft. long, 24-ft. wide, and 10-ft. high. Lighted from the top these are specially adapted for the exhibition of objects of interest, pictures, or for a local museum. A convenient residence for the Librarian is arranged in a separate building, which is extended so as to provide on the ground floor convenient rooms for the reception and storing of books and for the special work of the Librarians.

When the Library was first removed to the Assembly Rooms, the premises were leased from the States, who had purchased them in 1870. Subsequently, however, in December, 1883, Messrs. Guille and Allès purchased the Rooms from the States for £900 British, and afterwards bought from the Parish the plot of land behind the Rooms—which belonged to the Rectory—and upon which they have now built the spacious new premises above-mentioned. As soon as these extensions are available, the founders purpose inaugurating comprehensive courses of popular illustrated lectures on physical science, economic products, natural history, mi[Pg 38]croscopic science, literary subjects, &c., which will appeal at once to the eye and the understanding, and impart a large amount of very useful knowledge in an easy and agreeable way. There will also be classes in various subjects, including the French, German and Italian languages, drawing, music, &c., &c., all of which will be open to girls as well as boys, women as well as men. In an island like Guernsey, where from the smallness of the community many of the young people necessarily have to go and seek their fortunes abroad, the advantages for self-culture offered by an Institution like this can scarcely be over-rated. The local facilities afforded for the acquisition of French are particularly marked, while it cannot for a moment be doubted that a young man or woman who can use both French and English with fluency, is much better equipped for the battle of life than is a person knowing only one of these languages. Whatever intellectual needs may become apparent in the people, these the Guille-Allès Library will set itself to supply. Its founders, indeed, are especially anxious that there should be no hard and fast barriers about its settlement, which might cramp its expansion or fetter its usefulness. On the contrary they desire—while adhering, of course, to certain main lines of intellectual activity—to imbue it with such elasticity of adaptation as will enable it to successfully grapple with the changing necessities of changing times. The chief wants of to-day may not necessarily be the most pressing requisites of a century hence. Therefore, one of the greatest essentials—and at the same time one of the greatest difficulties—in a foundation like this, is to provide for and combine within it such a fixity of principle and such an adaptability of administration as shall enable it to keep pace with the progress of the ages, and suit itself to the several requirements of succeeding generations as they pass.

COST AND ENDOWMENT.

The cost of carrying out this great enterprise—including the erection of buildings, purchase of books, fittings, &c.—has already amounted to between £15,000 and £20,000,[Pg 39] and the outlay shows no signs of cessation. In addition to these expenses there is the Endowment Fund already referred to, and for this the munificent donors intend to set apart a sum to which the above amount bears but a small proportion. So that altogether the community will be indebted to them for an educational foundation worth a magnificent figure in money value alone, while besides this, we must not forget the long years of thoughtful care and of self-denying energy involved in maturing these splendid projects, or the healthy mental and moral stimulus which the conduct of these patriotic gentlemen has supplied.

PRESENTATION OF PORTRAITS.

A very pleasing ceremony took place on Wednesday, December 17th, 1884, at St. Julian's Hall, when His Excellency Major-General Sarel, C.B., Lieut.-Governor, presented Messrs. Guille and Allès with their portraits on behalf of a numerous body of subscribers resident in all parts of the island, and also in Paris, New York, and Brooklyn. A public meeting had been called on the 4th of February previous, when an influential Committee was appointed; about £227 was speedily raised, and then Mr. Frank Brooks was commissioned to paint two life-size portraits in oil, which gave great satisfaction when finished, and are now hung in the Library. Julius Carey, Esq., Chief Constable (Mayor) of St. Peter-Port, as President of the Portrait Committee, opened the proceedings, by briefly narrating the circumstances which had called the meeting together.

His Excellency then, after a few preliminary remarks, said:—

He must express the very great pleasure which he felt in being present on such an interesting occasion, when the whole community were testifying their appreciation of the noble Library which had been founded for their benefit. Indeed he felt it a great honour to have been asked to present these handsome portraits to Messrs. Guille and Allès. It would not be necessary for him to dwell at any length on the antecedents of these gentlemen, who were well-known in the island. Many years ago Mr. Guille went to the United States, and there he found the advantages which accrued from having access to a good library. He then conceived the idea of one day bestowing a[Pg 40] similar boon upon his own native island, and this project he had been happily spared to carry out. During his exile the thought had remained ever with him; he had not allowed business to engross all his attention; and now that he had returned once more to settle down in the little rock-bound island-home of his youth, he was reducing to practice the beneficent plans of earlier years. He was not content to lead a life of ease with the produce of his industry, but he had founded an institution of incalculable value for the moral and intellectual welfare of the isle. Then there was another large-hearted Guernseyman, Mr. Allès, who determined that his old friend Mr. Guille should not be left to carry out his noble scheme alone. They had long been associated in business enterprises, and they were now linked in the higher bond of a common desire for the well-being of their fellow-citizens. All honour to them for it. The Library told its own story and needed no encomium. All it wanted was constant readers and plenty of them, and he could not too strongly impress upon the people—and especially upon the rising generation—the immense advantages they would derive from availing themselves of its literary treasures. In conclusion, it simply remained for him, on behalf of the Committee and the Subscribers, to ask Messrs. Guille and Allès to accept these paintings, which would show to future generations of Guernseymen the form and features of two public benefactors who had deserved so well of their country and their kind.

Mr. Guille, in response, gave a very interesting address in English, and Mr. Allès followed with an equally appropriate and practical speech in French, both gentlemen being received with prolonged applause, and listened to by the numerous assembly with the most interested attention.

Brief complimentary addresses were then delivered by Edgar MacCulloch, Esq., F.S.A., Bailiff (Chief Magistrate) of Guernsey, and by F.J. Jeremie, Esq., M.A., Jurat of the Royal Court, and the proceedings terminated with a hearty vote of thanks to the Lieut.-Governor, proposed by the Very Rev. Carey Brock, M.A., Dean of Guernsey.

A brass plate attached to Mr. Guille's portrait bears the following inscription:—

Presented to THOMAS GUILLE, Esq.,
by his numerous friends, in recognition of the great
benefit he has conferred upon the inhabitants of his
native Island as one of the Founders of the
Guille-Allès Library.

Guernsey, 17 December, 1884.

A similar plate, bearing the name of Mr. Frederick Mansell Allès, is attached to his portrait.

Note.—The Assembly Rooms were built by private subscription in 1782, at a cost of about £2,500, and had therefore been in existence exactly a century when they passed into the hands of Messrs. Guille and Allès in 1882. During this long period they were the fashionable *foyer* of the Island's festivity and gaiety, and formed the scene of many a brilliant gathering.

www.ingramcontent.com/pod-product-compliance
Lightning Source LLC
LaVergne TN
LVHW051710080426
835511LV00017B/2835